Original title:
Astrophysical Anecdotes

Copyright © 2025 Creative Arts Management OÜ
All rights reserved.

Author: Julian Prescott
ISBN HARDBACK: 978-1-80567-781-9
ISBN PAPERBACK: 978-1-80567-902-8

Stellar Reflections in a Cosmic Sea

Stars in the sky, oh what a sight,
Twinkling like diamonds, shining bright.
But if they could talk, oh what they'd say,
"Stop staring at us, go out and play!"

Planets in orbits, a dance so fine,
"Hey, Earth, don't forget to sip your wine!"
Gravity giggles at all our fuss,
"Chill out, human, you're part of us!"

Comet's Farewell

A comet zoomed by, with a tail so bold,
"Catch me if you can," it cheekily told.
But as it sped off into the night,
"I forgot my wallet! Now that's not right!"

Stardust behind it, a glimmering trail,
"Did you see that guy? He'll never fail!"
He waved goodbye in a dazzling arc,
Leaving us laughing in the dark.

A Sonnet for Supernova

A supernova popped, quite the surprise,
"Look at me now," it said with a rise.
"Don't blink too fast, I'm here for a show,
But watch your toes; I'm destined to blow!"

"Popcorn in the sky—who needs a theater?
I'll light up the night with a burst, nothing sweeter!"
Galaxies watch with wide-open eyes,
As this brilliant star has its grand goodbyes.

Journal of a Wandering Pulsar

Dear diary, today, I spun for a thrill,
Tick-tock on the clock, what a crazy skill!
The cosmos applauded, a standing ovation,
As I twirled like a star, a cosmic sensation.

But oh, those black holes—they're so out of line!
"Why don't you join me? We'll have a fine dine!"
"Can't slow me down, I'm too cool for that,"
I winked at the galaxy, and tipped my hat.

Celestial Forgiveness in Orbit

A comet sneezed, it made a mess,
Caught our planet in its dress.
The rings of Saturn laughed so loud,
While Jupiter rolled deep in a cloud.

Mars dropped its ice cream on the ground,
The Milky Way giggled without a sound.
Stars whispered secrets, oh so bright,
Making black holes snicker out of sight.

Celestial Shadows and Sunrises

The sun lost its way and hit a star,
Now it calls itself a cosmic czar.
Planets chuckle at the strange parade,
Shadows dancing, cosmic charade.

Venus tripped over a space-time line,
Laughed it off, said, "I'm still divine!"
Eclipses grinned, they planned a show,
While Earth's just trying to steal the glow.

Stargazer's Chronicles

A stargazer slipped on a moonbeam slide,
Fell right into a black hole wide.
Planets stopped to witness this fun,
"Guess his adventure's just begun!"

Distant quasars wink with delight,
As telescopes squabble over the sight.
With every blink, a story spins,
Of aliens laughing at our sins.

The Quiet Revolution of Stardust

In a nebula, dust bunnies collide,
With starlight giggles, they don't hide.
Supernova's throwing a disco ball,
While asteroids come to have a ball.

Galaxies swap their favorite tunes,
As meteors dance under the moons.
Each twinkle tells a playful tale,
Of space shenanigans that never pale.

Cosmic Ballet of the Planets

In a dance of orbs, they twirl with glee,
Mars stepped on Mercury, now that's quite funny!
Saturn lost a ring, it rolled down with a clink,
Jupiter laughed loud, causing a cosmic wink.

Venus tripped on clouds, and her makeup was smeared,
Pluto threw a party, though no one appeared.
All the stars giggled, they mocked the big sun,
As space jammed to tunes — the cosmos had fun!

The Tremor of Eclipsed Souls

The moon played peek-a-boo, with the day glowing bright,
Sun threw a tantrum, quite a hilarious sight.
Stars juggled their twinkles and slipped on the dew,
While comets cracked jokes, racing fast like a crew.

Earth shook with laughter, a tremor of cheer,
Shooting stars winked, as if whispering near.
Galaxies swayed, laughing silently so,
In this cosmic comedy show, stars steal the show!

The Pulse of Space and Time

Tick-tock went the cosmos, a clock in delight,
Time tripped on starlight, oh what a sight!
Black holes made faces, sucking in all the fun,
While wormholes played hopscotch, just to outrun.

Galactic giggles ricocheted off the void,
Echoes of laughter — oh how they enjoyed!
Photons raced by, full of energy and cheer,
The pulse of the universe, simply crystal clear!

Celestial Dreams in the Dark

In the dark of the night, stars plotted a scheme,
 Uranus told jokes, it made everyone beam.
  A nebula yawned, its colors in a swirl,
 While meteorites danced, to a cosmic twirl.

Dreams drift in silence, giggling softly along,
  The void hums a tune, a curious song.
 Lunar laughter echoed, in this vast, silly park,
Creating celestial dreams in the whimsical dark!

Tales from the Event Horizon

A black hole sneezed, light years away,
All the stars started to sway.
Asteroids danced, no rhythm in sight,
Planets were giggling in sheer delight.

Caught in the pull of a cosmic prank,
Satellites floated like boats on a tank.
Gravity chuckled, a teasing old thing,
As meteors juggled and comets took wing.

Celestial Cartographer's Diary

Drawn on a map with spaghetti strands,
My planets fell over, they didn't understand.
Every line wobbly, a cosmic cuisine,
Saturn wore rings of bad engineering.

Uranus laughed loudly, said 'What's this mess?'
'You call this a map? It's a total distress!'
Stars in confusion, they twinkled and frowned,
Navigational skills are nowhere to be found.

The Gravity of Lost Time

Time slipped away like a slippery fish,
I wished for a moment, just one silly wish.
But gravity giggled, said 'Not on my watch!'
And whirlpooled my plans, such a dastardly botch.

A clock struck twelve, but it wasn't the same,
Each hour was bouncy, a laughable game.
Time travelers tripped, fell into a twirl,
Kicked by black holes, they sent me to whirl.

Starlit Stories of the Unheard

In the quiet of night, a star started to snore,
Big bang noises echoing, a galactic roar.
Clouds chuckled softly, covering their eyes,
As meteors winked like they held the best spies.

Aliens guffawed at a lackluster dance,
Those little green men had quite the chance.
They spun in the dark, with two left feet,
Creating a rhythm—oh, what a treat!

The Eternal Embrace of Black Holes

A cosmic vacuum with a playful grin,
It gobbles up stars like it's at a win.
You step too close, it says, "Come here, friend!"
And just like that, it's the universe's end.

Gravity's prankster, swirling in delight,
It whispers, "Don't worry, you'll be alright!"
But once you're inside, it's a one-way ride,
No return ticket for the event horizon tide.

Twilight Parables of the Universe

Stars gather round for a bedtime tale,
Of cosmic oddities that never grow stale.
The moon's got jokes, the sun's a big flirt,
In this galactic circus, nothing hurts.

Planets giggle as they spin around,
While comets dance, leaving trails profound.
"What's it like in your orbit?" one asks with glee,
"Just keep your space, or you might bump into me!"

Stars Whisper Secrets

In the night sky, secrets softly flow,
Stars giggle and wink, putting on a show.
"I'm older than you, but you shine so bright,"
"Just wait, little one, we'll burn out tonight."

Whispers of stardust cross vast cosmic seas,
"Did you hear that one about the redshift tease?"
As they twinkle with laughter, the universe sighs,
Every secret shared under inky dark skies.

The Dance of Celestial Bodies

Planets in tutus, they twirl with grace,
While meteors crash, just in case.
Galaxies twirl like they're at a ball,
Spinning around, they can't help but fall.

"Watch out for gravity!" the dancers all shout,
Laughter erupts as they swirl about.
In this cosmic ballet, they trip and collide,
But it's all in good fun, they take it in stride.

Dreams Suspended in Zero Gravity

In a rocket made of cheese,
Astronauts float with perfect ease,
Chasing stars that look like peas,
Their laughter heard upon the breeze.

They juggle planets, one by one,
Trying to prove they have some fun,
But floating snacks? It's never done,
As crumbs drift off 'til they are gone.

With zero G, they lose their grip,
Their drinks become a wobbly slip,
And as they coast on cosmic trips,
They laugh at how the soda whips.

So up they go, with dreams so wide,
In space, there's always room to hide,
In zero gravity, they confide,
A silly quest, a joyride glide.

The Silence Between Galaxies

In the void, it's quiet as a mouse,
Stars are gossiping, oh, what a rouse!
Feeling lonely, they start to grouse,
Until a comet dances through the house.

Black holes yawn, they pull their tricks,
While stardust settles in funny flicks,
Nebulae whisper, do cosmic licks,
As giggles echo in starry mix.

Planets spin like tops on a stage,
Bumping into each, in a cosmic rage,
Eventually, they flee, like a page,
From a book too wild for any age.

In this silence, laughter springs anew,
The galaxies share their jests so true,
Floating together in a space so blue,
Creating chaos, just for a view.

Time's Tapestry in the Cosmos

Woven threads of moments past,
The clock ticks slowly, but oh so fast,
Time travels sideways like a cast,
In constellations, memories are amassed.

Each second giggles as it flies,
One tick, two tock, under starry skies,
Elusive minutes slip like pies,
While space-time gives us cheerful highs.

Forget the past? Not when it laughs,
Chasing shadows, making quirky crafts,
In cosmic gardens, it slyly drafts,
Fun surprises from its playful halves.

When we peek at this time machine,
With its tangled yarns, oh so obscene,
The jokes it plays are rarely keen,
Yet in its grasp, we're always seen.

Reflections in an Astral Pool

Beneath the stars, a pool of light,
Rippling dreams in the endless night,
Fish with wings take joyful flight,
While ducks wear hats—what a sight!

The moon dips low, with a wink and grin,
As planets quiz on where they've been,
Jupiter's joke leaves Saturn in spin,
In this cosmic giggle, we all fit in.

Galactic waves, they splash and play,
Stars are rallying, come what may,
In this mirror, they dance and sway,
Sharing chuckles along the way.

Splash! A comet jumps with glee,
Water turns to laughter, can't you see?
In the astral pool, there's mischief free,
A cosmic joke, that's how it should be.

Shadows of the Milky Way

Stars twinkle like fireflies,
In a cosmic party, oh what a surprise!
A comet slips on its glowing tail,
While planets share secrets over ale.

Moon forgot his lines in the show,
Jupiter laughed, 'You steal the glow!'
Galaxies dance in a swirling spree,
Asteroids crash, 'Oops! Sorry me!'

Fragmented Light: A Celestial Journey

Light beams wander, taking their time,
One gets lost in a solar rhyme.
Photons play hide and seek at night,
While black holes say, 'Not in my sight!'

A shooting star trips on its own flare,
Twisting like it just don't care.
Nebulas giggle, forming a haze,
While supernovas pop in a daze.

The Birth of a Nebula

In a cradle of gas, sparkles ignite,
Dust bunnies form a chaotic night.
Whispers of color so bright and bold,
They thought they'd start a nebula fold.

A passing star winks, 'Don't take it too fast,'
But the dust clouds chuckle, 'We're built to last!'
Coming together, they spin with glee,
Creating a spectacle, oh what a spree!

Tales from the Astral Shore

On cosmic sands, aliens tread light,
Building castles, oh what a sight!
Shooting stars race with laughter proclaimed,
While Neptune plays tag, ever unclaimed.

A voice from behind yells, 'Watch where you step!'
But Saturn just laughs, 'This is a rep!'
With rings and a grin, it joins the fray,
Sipping stardust cocktails by the bay.

Celestial Whispers Beneath the Stars

A comet dressed in polka dots,
It twirls and spins, a show it flaunts.
The planets laugh in cosmic jest,
While meteors claim to be the best.

Galaxies gossip, swirling bright,
'Who does that sun think it can ignite?'
With starlit banter, they play all night,
In the cosmic sea, there's no end in sight.

Saturn grins, its rings on display,
While Mars throws confetti, oh what a day!
They kick up dust, a heavenly grime,
As comets whistle tunes, keeping time.

Through telescopes, folks munch on snacks,
As aliens giggle, exchanging quacks.
In this stellar circus, fun's the game,
Where laughter echoes, and stars have names.

Ink of the Universe Scribbles

The universe writes with a cosmic pen,
Doodles of stars, again and again.
Black holes swirl, like ink in a glass,
Creating chaos in interstellar class.

Jupiter's stripes, like a fashion trend,
Droplets of space, where galaxies bend.
Wormholes giggle, as they bend the rules,
Skipping through time like mischievous fools.

While quasars tweet in stellar chirps,
Venus sighs, wearing sparkly burps.
Pulsars blink with playful zest,
While Earth rolls its eyes, "I'll need a rest!"

Each star a story, dripped in delight,
Spilling secrets throughout the night.
The ink of cosmos, wild and free,
Makes scribblers of us, you and me.

Fantasies of the Universe Wrapped in Light

A star in a turtleneck, cozy and bright,
Hums a soft tune that dances in flight.
Black holes chuckle, swirling spaghetti,
While moons play leapfrog, oh so ready!

Satellites toss and spin on a whim,
As they twirl around like kids on a rim.
Pulsating light, a disco ball's glee,
Makes this far-off realm feel like a spree.

Asteroids play tag, zooming around,
In the cosmic park, no worries abound.
The sun's golden rays, a spotlight fine,
On this fantastical stage, we all intertwine.

In laughter and joy, the universe spins,
While stardust grins, embracing its wins.
With each twinkling wink, a wish takes flight,
In the grand play of life, everything's bright.

Memories Wrapped in Light

Oh look, a star with a wobbly hue,
It danced at night, who knew it could screw!
A comet sneezed and left a trail,
While Mars just sat, sipping space ale.

The moon forgot where it had to be,
Tripped on a cloud, oh how carefree!
Jupiter's storms served as its hairdo,
And Saturn winked, saying, "Hey, good view!"

The Poetry of Celestial Lines

I wrote a poem on a shooting star,
But it zoomed away, now I'm left ajar.
Venus chuckled, 'You missed your chance!'
As it twirled around in a bubble dance.

A black hole once pulled my pen into space,
'Why so serious?' it asked with a face.
While I just laughed at the cosmic game,
Knowing the stars play just the same!

A Symphony of Celestial Cries

A meteor shower sang out a tune,
But all I heard was a cosmic goon.
Neptune looked on with a watery grin,
'How's that for music? Did you hear the din?'

Galaxies twirled like a wild ballet,
While asteroids fought for the brightest display.
With supernovae giggling at their plight,
They danced through the void, laughter taking flight.

The Secrets in the Cosmos' Breath

The universe whispered secrets so bright,
'Have you seen Pluto? It's off the invite!'
Stars play poker, and guess who's bluffing?
A debate with gravity, that keeps on puffing.

Aliens dropped by just to have fun,
But forgot to take back their cheesy stun gun.
With a wink they exclaimed, 'Earth, what a view!'
As they zipped off, shouting, 'We'll miss you too!'

Reflections on a Lunar Lake

On a lake of silver light,
Frogs sing to the moon so bright,
They leap like astronauts at play,
In a splash of cosmic ballet.

A fish with stars in its eyes,
Tells a tale of alien skies,
Wonders if it should wear a suit,
To meet those folks from the astute.

The water ripples with laughter,
As space whales swim in a slumber,
Crickets chirp with galactic glee,
Plotting journeys on a spree.

With each wave, echoes resume,
Splashy jokes in lunar gloom,
One last leap before the dawn,
They wave goodbye, to sleep on.

Wormholes of the Heart

In love's distorted space-time,
Two hearts spin in prose and rhyme,
Finding paths through cosmic strife,
Crossing lines to find true life.

A comet passes with a wink,
"Are you sure?" it starts to think,
In orbits both bizarre and grand,
Seeking connections hand in hand.

Misguided meteors collide,
In a dance they cannot hide,
One sighs, "Let's not drift apart!"
Navigating wormholes of the heart.

Black holes gulping down sweet chance,
In the cosmos, they'll still dance,
Spinning tales that make you shout,
Finding love's path, without a doubt.

The Celestial Clockwork

A sassy sun with burning flair,
Tick-tocks time with solar flare,
Planets march like little clocks,
In a row of space odd socks.

Mercury is always late,
In meetings with the cosmic fate,
Venus giggles, dressed in gold,
Wonders if it's time to fold.

"Let's take a break!" the Saturn shouts,
With rings that twirl and wiggle about,
Jupiter's mass debates the rules,
While Mars brings snacks, just for fools.

In this machinery of fun,
Every tick tells a joke spun,
Galaxies pulse, a great big laugh,
In the universe's goofy graph.

Star Maps of the Unseen

In the attic of the night,
Star maps whisper, taking flight,
They pull out tricks and old routines,
With laughter echoing through the scenes.

Twinkle, twinkle, little star,
Lost your way? Not very far!
Just ask a comet for a ride,
In this cosmic joyride slide.

Aliens peeking through the charts,
With doodles of interstellar arts,
Sketching dreams with a smirk,
On spaceships where they lurk.

Navigating trails of dust,
With giggles, they frame their trust,
For every map has tales unheard,
In the vastness, joy's preferred.

The Symphony of Celestial Orbits

In a dance where planets twirl,
Saturn drops its rings, oh, what a whirl!
Mars just giggles, saying, "Look at me!"
While Earth waves, sipping her cup of tea.

The moons all chuckle, making a scene,
Jupiter's storms are a mess, it's obscene!
Venus blushes, thinking she's the star,
But the comet zooms by, saying, "Not so far!"

A stellar orchestra plays in the sky,
As meteor showers appear up high.
The black holes whisper, 'Swallow some light!'
While galaxies play tag all through the night.

So let's not forget in our cosmic quest,
That space is amusing, and we're but guests.
With each orbit spinning in silly delight,
The universe laughs beneath the starlight.

Rapture of the Red Dwarf

Oh little red dwarf, so shy and so small,
You joke with the giants and laugh with them all.
You say, "I'm compact, but I shine just the same!"
While nearby supernovas are busy with fame.

Caught in your glow, the planets all spin,
Yet they often wonder, "Where do we fit in?"
The asteroids chuckle as they drift past your door,
"We're just here for snacks, who could ask for more?"

Your fusion is low, but still you ignite,
As the sun grins down, day and night.
You're the underdog star in this cosmic game,
And we love you dearly, red dwarf is your name.

So let's pop some popcorn and watch you shine,
In a galactic comedy, how you will dine!
Your tiny fire keeping us all entertained,
A sparkling jester, ever unchained.

Whispers of the Ancient Pulsar

Hey there, pulsar, with your beams so bright,
You twirl like a dancer, in the dark of the night.
You tick and you tock, a cosmic clock,
With every rotation, you send a shock.

While galaxies swirl with such grace and ease,
You slay with your rhythm, like a cosmic tease.
"Who needs a partner when I shine so divine?"
Echoes your laughter across space and time.

Neutron stars shaking, trying to impress,
But you just wink, saying, "I must confess,
I'm the life of the party, the light in the deep,
What's a little gravity? I still hear you weep!"

Your ancient stories float on solar winds,
As black holes chuckle, knowing where it begins.
With every pulse, you tell tales so grand,
Of universes far—come, take my hand!

Shadows on a Solar Canvas

Colors splash across the solar sphere,
Planets with brushes paint where they steer.
Mercury giggles, 'Too hot to stay!'
While Neptune huffs, "I'm just too far away!"

Eclipses get nervous, 'Will we block the sun?'
While stardust dances, saying, "Aren't we fun?"
The sun says, "Shadows? Oh, bring them near,
We'll play hide and seek! Who's got the fear?"

Uranus spins, sporting a funny hat,
While comets race by, 'Chase me, just like that!'
The stars all twinkle, adding to the mix,
Creating a canvas with playful tricks.

From dusk to dawn, the sky is alive,
With laughter and wonder, we all arrive.
So grab your brushes, join in the game,
In this cosmic art show, we're all the same!

The Dance of Dust and Light

In the cosmos, dust took flight,
Twinkling under starlit night.
It swirled and twirled with great delight,
Making even black holes look polite.

A nebula winks, what a sight!
"Aren't we fabulous?" it said, quite right.
A duster in hand, it shines so bright,
While planets giggle at the cosmic fright.

The sun threw a party, oh what a tease!
While planets danced, swaying in the breeze.
They tripped on a meteor, fell to their knees,
And laughed while dodging space dust with ease.

The comets stopped by, what a hoot!
Spinning tales of cosmic pursuit.
With laughter and joy, they did delight,
In the grand ballet of dust and light.

When Comets Weep

When comets weep, they leave a trail,
Of giggles, sparkles, without fail.
They cry from joy, not from the scale,
Leaving the universe to exhale.

Galaxies sigh, 'Oh, what a show!'
As comets fly by, moving to and fro.
They whisper jokes, oh don't you know?
With every laugh, their tails aglow.

One comet said, 'I lost my way!'
Shooting stars laughed, 'Let's joke and play!'
Forget the map, just seize the day,
In cosmic tumble, we all can sway.

The universe chuckled, full of cheer,
As comets pranced, far and near.
In their weeping, joy appeared,
Creating laughter in the sphere.

Luminiferous Dreams

In dreams of light, the stars conspire,
To dance on whims of cosmic fire.
They gear up for a wild attire,
With photons ready, they never tire.

A quasar wore a feathery hat,
While black holes whispered, "Imagine that!"
Shooting stars played a game of chat,
Creating ripples, how about that?

Supernovae boomed, 'Now we're the hype!'
As galaxies swayed in a cosmic type.
They joked they'd form a stellar stripe,
Painting the void in a playful swipe.

With bright reflectors, they made it clear,
In dreams of light, there's nothing to fear.
As laughter echoed throughout the sphere,
The universe beamed, full of cheer.

Orbits of Forgotten Stars

In orbits wild, the stars did roam,
Forgotten tales of their home.
They giggled softly, in cosmic foam,
Crafting myths they'd like to comb.

One said, 'Oh dear, I lost my shine!'
A friend replied, 'Let's make it fine!'
With stardust sprinkled like a brine,
They laughed so hard, feeling divine.

Around the Milky Way they spun,
Telling stories of ancient fun.
Their light dimmed, but oh, what a run!
Reviving laughter, never done.

So if you look up in the night,
Remember the stars in their playful plight.
Forgotten gems, shining so bright,
In the cosmic theater, what a sight!

The First Light of Creation

In the void, where silence lay,
A star sneezed, and blew us away.
Galaxies spun, all in a rush,
And comets danced, causing a hush.

Planets played peek-a-boo at night,
Too shy to shine, they ducked from light.
But the moon, oh such a tease,
Winked down at us with cosmic ease.

Nebulas puffed clouds of paint,
In colors that would make one faint.
While black holes played hide and seek,
And gravity gave us quite the peek.

A supernova threw a party to end,
With fireworks that nobody could fend.
And as we watched, joyful and bold,
We laughed at the stories they told.

Discord in the Celestial Choir

Stars gathered for a concert grand,
But forgot their notes, oh isn't that bland!
Nebulas sang like cats in a fight,
While comets crashed, creating a fright.

The sun tried to lead with a radiant gleam,
But tripped on a beat, fell into a dream.
Sparks flew, a cosmic mess was made,
As planets laughed—what a grand charade!

Jupiter boomed with a laugh so deep,
While Saturn twirled, making rings that sweep.
But Mercury honked, his horns misplayed,
And all the stars blushed, utterly swayed.

Finally, the moon chimed in so sly,
"Let's just jam; why not? Oh my!"
So they played on, in their disorderly way,
Staying up late, to dance and sway.

Hunting for Celestial Treasures

On a quest in the swirls of night,
We searched for gems, all sparkly and bright.
But found a rock that was just a dud,
Maybe next time, we'll skip the mud.

Mercury giggled, "I hid some gold!"
Yet all we spotted was space-age mold.
Venus shrugged, flashing her dazzling sheen,
Promising riches that just can't be seen.

We dived through the dust of a cosmic cave,
Chasing illusions that made us behave.
With asteroids laughing at us in jest,
We left empty-handed from this strange quest.

But oh, the fun of our wild chase!
Even clouds joined in the wild race.
So who needs treasure when we've got this?
Each giggle and snicker is pure heavenly bliss!

Fables of the Fading Light

Once upon a time, in a sky so vast,
A star blinked twice, and then faded fast.
The universe sighed, "Oh what a shame!
Let's turn it into a ghostly game."

Planets gathered, sharing tales in glow,
Of missing lights, and what they might show.
"Did the star trip?" one wondered aloud,
"We should have made it wear something proud!"

Now comets float, like wisps of hair,
Drifting through cosmos without a care.
While black holes chuckle, pulling the charm,
Each flicker of light adding to the warm.

So when you gaze at the stars up high,
Remember the tale of the fading sky.
For even in darkness, we'll always find,
A spark of laughter, lighthearted and kind.

When the Sun Spoke

One day the Sun said, 'Hey, look at me!'
I shine so bright, can't you see?
But every planet rolled their eyes,
'We can't hear you, with those solar cries!'

The stars laughed hard, twinkling their lights,
'Oh, dear Sun, you think you're so bright!'
But whispers travel across the vast space,
It's hard to catch when you're out of place.

Radiating rays with stories to tell,
The Sun stood proud, ready to yell.
But cosmic winds kept blowing him down,
Making the other stars laugh and frown.

So next time you feel like you're the one,
Remember the tale of the chatterbox Sun.
Sometimes it's laughter that lights up the sky,
Not just bright flames in the universe high.

The Solitude of Meteor Showers

Meteor showers, they come and go,
Falling stars at the midnight show.
Each rock whispers, 'Grant me a wish!'
But they get burned, oh, what a dish!

They streak through dark with quite a flair,
Leaving behind their cosmic hair.
Yet in their speed, they seek embrace,
Alas, they vanish—oh, such a race!

Once one shouted, 'Don't let me fall!'
And the other replied, 'We're having a ball!'
But as they zipped past our blue sphere,
Too fast for wishes, what a real fear!

So if you spot them in the night,
Wave goodbye to their speedy flight.
For in their solitude, they might despair,
Or laugh, at the tales flung through the air.

Diving into Cosmic Whirlpools

There once was a comet, sleek and spry,
Diving through galaxies, oh, how he'd fly!
He spun in whirlpools, round and around,
Yelling, 'Hold tight! This life's profound!'

The planets gawked, some shouted with glee,
'Is that a comet, or could it be?
A cosmic dancer, swooping so low,
He's gone in a blink—where did he go?'

But round and round, he would twirl and chase,
Daring the universe at a dizzying pace.
Yet, gravity whispered, 'Stay in your lane!'
But our comet just laughed, calling it vain.

So, if you see a streak in the night,
Just know it's a comet in magical flight.
Diving through whirlpools, feeling the zest,
Knowing that cosmic laughter is best!

The Soul's Orbit

In the dance of stars, the soul found a groove,
Orbiting laughter, making quite a move.
It twirled past comets, light as a breeze,
Singing with planets, 'Oh, won't you please?'

Moonbeams tickled, in the soft glow,
The soul wiggled out, putting on a show.
'Come join the party!' it whimsically said,
But the Milky Way yawned, still half in bed.

Through clusters and dust, it spun with delight,
'Caught up in the magic of galactic night.'
Yet each time it stopped, oh what a sight,
Finding new friends in the endless flight.

So when in the cosmos, don't lose your cheer,
The soul's little giggle brings joy far and near.
In the grand space of laughter, take your chance—
For in every orbit lies a whimsical dance!

Celestial Whispers

Once a comet waved its tail,
And slipped upon a cosmic scale.
The stars giggled in delight,
While planets danced through the night.

A black hole took a silly leap,
And swallowed up a galaxy's sheep.
The moons chuckled at the sight,
As they wobbled with pure delight.

Supernovae threw a party wide,
Inviting all from each side.
But little did they know it's true,
They'd end up exploding too!

The Milky Way played hide and seek,
In spiral arms so sly and sleek.
But when the sun turned round to frown,
It accidentally spilled its crown.

Starborn Secrets

A star once whispered low and sweet,
To an astronaut lost in heat.
But the signal got all tangled tight,
Said, "Can you hear me? I'm out of sight!"

A twinkle learned to dance one day,
And led a whole comet ballet.
With glittering moves, they twirled around,
'Til a supernova burst, and wow, what a sound!

Moons held a contest for the best spin,
While asteroids tried not to give in.
But one little rock fell flat on its face,
And became the punchline of space's own grace.

The sun wore shades to feel real cool,
While planets played tag, breaking each rule.
They laughed until the shadows grew,
And called it a day by twilight's cue.

The Cosmic Tale of Wandering Planets

Once a planet tried to roam,
But missed its way back home.
It bumped into a shooting star,
And asked, "Hey, do you know where we are?"

Two giants had an arm-wrestle grand,
But tripped on dust and lost their stand.
They rolled through space laughing in glee,
While moons cheered, enviously free.

A little blue world lost its hat,
Chasing it across the cosmic mat.
But the wind was wild, and off it flew,
Settling on a Martian brew!

Jupiter's storms threw a wild affair,
They invited all for a ride through air.
But when the fun finally hit a peak,
It rained down laughter, what a cheek!

Echoes of Distant Galaxies

In the far reaches where light does fade,
Galaxies play their own charade.
They whisper jokes in cosmic hue,
Echoes of laughter, perceptions askew.

A pulsar with a rhythm so bold,
Played a tune that never grew old.
While black holes tried to spin along,
But got lost in the cosmic throng.

Each supercluster told a tale,
Of starry brawls and intergalactic mail.
Yet none could recall where they came from,
Just echoes of laughter, a starry hum.

As all the comets played tag with the sun,
They shouted, "Chase me! Oh, this is fun!"
And when night fell, their glow so bright,
Left the universe smiling with delight.

Milky Way's Midnight Tales

Stars danced like clowns, full of cheer,
Darkness giggled, nothing to fear.
A comet slipped on cosmic ice,
Said, 'This isn't my first paradise!'

Planets played hide and seek in the void,
Jupiter yelled, 'I'm not overjoyed!'
Mars fell in love with a passing satellite,
But Venus just laughed, 'You'll never get it right!'

The Veil of the Aurora

Lights twirled above in a pulsing show,
Saying, 'We're here for a cosmic glow!'
Neon fish swam in the shimmering air,
As if the sky just had a hair flair!

Aliens waved from the stars so bright,
Sporting new shades, looking quite right.
'Join us,' they said, 'in our disco ball!'
'We only accept those who can have a ball!'

Echoes of a Lost Galaxy

Whispers floated from a black hole's grin,
It shouted, 'You can't take me in!'
Lost galaxies giggled, spinning about,
'Tell us a secret, we want them stout!'

A supernova burst with a juicy joke,
'Why did the star hide? It was all cloak!'
Dust sighed, 'Is this the end of the show?'
But it just laughed, 'We've got more in tow!'

Cosmic Threads Weaving Fate

In the loom of time, stars knit and tangle,
Sewing destinies, a cosmic wrangle.
A nebula sneezed, caused a great splash,
Creating a planet that looked like a mustache!

Galaxies giggled, their laughter resounds,
As quasars twirl with their playful bounds.
They said, 'We're here for a celestial game!'
While black holes joked, 'We're all a bit lame!'

The Enigmas of Celestial Whirls

In the cosmos, what a sight,
Stars dance away, what a delight!
Planets trip on invisible lines,
While comets giggle in cosmic designs.

A black hole's laugh, deep and loud,
Swallowing light, it's quite the crowd!
Galaxies spin like a merry-go-round,
Asteroids stumble, never on solid ground.

Supernovae, a bright flash of fun,
Leaving gas clouds for everyone!
Meteor showers shoot through the night,
Giggling stars, oh what a sight!

In the end, we all collide,
With laughter echoing far and wide.
Glue in space, with humor we soar,
In the vastness, there's always more!

When Planets Collide in Silence

Two planets met, oh what a sight,
They didn't shout, not a bit of fright.
Bumping gently, like kids at play,
"What was that?" they'd giggle away.

Saturn spun in a ringed disguise,
Jupiter chuckled in clouded skies.
Asteroids joined in a wobbly dance,
Stumbling over in cosmic chance.

Neptune whispered secrets to the Moon,
"Let's prank the Earth, let's sing a tune!"
But Earth just rolled her eyes with grace,
"Please, not another planet chase!"

So in silence, they all collide,
With stellar silliness as their guide.
A galactic giggle, a friendly press,
In this universe, we're all a mess!

A Celestial Diary of Dust

Once upon a stellar night,
Dust bunnies gathered, what a sight!
Writing tales and laughing loud,
In the cosmos, they felt so proud.

Asteroids sharing their biggest fears,
While stardust giggled, wiping tears.
"Remember that time we got lost in space?"
"Let's just say we'll keep our pace!"

Galactic gossip over cups of light,
Star fibers twinkled, oh what a flight!
They sketch the tales, with ink of glow,
Creating legends, a cosmic show.

So each night, the diary grows,
With funny stories that nobody knows.
In the vast expanse where stars gather round,
It's laughter and light that truly astound!

The Cosmic Tides of Us

Riding waves of lunar glow,
The tides of humor ebb and flow.
Stars laugh softly, as they partake,
In cosmic pranks, oh for heaven's sake!

A celestial beach, where comets play,
Stranded meteors, "Not today!"
The sun grins wide, his rays so bold,
"Let's tell the planets what we told!"

The moon holds secrets, a wink in the night,
"Did you see Earth's dance? It was quite the sight!"
With tides of laughter, the galaxies swell,
In this cosmic play, all's well that sells.

So let us float on this astral sea,
Where laughter's gravity pulls gently.
In this universe, don't you fuss,
We ride the waves, for it's the tides of us!

Echoes from the Cosmic Void

In the void, a joke took flight,
Sent from a star, shining bright.
A neutron walked into a bar,
Said, "I'm not charged, but who you are?"

The black holes laughed, they couldn't eat,
Singularity jokes, always a treat.
Quasars giggled, light-years away,
Tickling time, making it sway.

Galaxies spun in a dizzying twirl,
Sharing punchlines with a cosmic whirl.
The universe snickered, stars did chime,
Laughter echoing through space and time.

So if you gaze into the night sky,
Remember, even stars can be sly.
For in every twinkle, whimsy might dwell,
A cosmic laugh, a far-off tale to tell.

Tales of the Wandering Stars

Once upon a time in the skies,
Stars debated, oh what a prize!
One said, "I shine more than you!"
The other shot back, "I'm a planet too!"

They raced through orbits, sweet celestial feud,
One tripped on a comet, landing quite rude.
The moon just chuckled, holding her light,
"You all look silly, it's quite the sight!"

A shooting star slipped, fell from grace,
"I should've practiced my landing space!"
But laughter erupted all through the night,
Wandering stars sharing giggles of light.

So next time you wish on a twinkling flare,
Remember those stars, giggling in air.
In the vastness above, humor ignites,
A tapestry woven from whimsical sights.

When Nebulas Breathe

In cosmic clouds, the colors blend,
Nebulas chuckle, and then they send.
"What do you call a star with no light?"
A dark comedy, oh what a fright!

They puff out gas, then sneeze with flair,
Creating new worlds with laughter to share.
Asteroids rolling, they tremble and shake,
"Did you hear that one? It's a big mistake!"

The swirling mists spin jokes all night,
While little stars twinkle with delight.
In every puff, a giggle escapes,
Sketching joy's form, no need for capes.

So when you see colors painted in space,
Know that behind them, there's a merry place.
For nebulas breathe with humor divine,
Painting the cosmos with laughter's design.

The Gravity of Forgotten Dreams

In a world where dreams seem to fall,
Gravity giggles, it hears them all.
"Why can't dreams just fly away?"
"Because I'm here, at least for today!"

Astronauts floating with wild, crazy schemes,
Try to catch laughter, pull in their dreams.
But the moon chimes in, "You're all just too slow!"
"Try harder, dear friends, let laughter go!"

Planets were plotting some humorous pranks,
Jupiter's belly, they all gave thanks.
"I'm full of jokes, come and take a bite!"
But Saturn just said, "Let's dance tonight!"

So as you ponder those dreams left to roam,
Remember the laughter that echoes like foam.
For even in gravity's heavy embrace,
The dreams find a way to float with grace.

www.ingramcontent.com/pod-product-compliance
Lightning Source LLC
Chambersburg PA
CBHW071813160426
43209CB00003B/71